drug facts
MARIJUANA

TED GOTTFRIED with Lisa Harkrader

Marshall Cavendish
Benchmark
New York

Marshall Cavendish Benchmark
99 White Plains Road
Tarrytown, NY 10591
www.marshallcavendish.us

Library of Congress Cataloging-in-Publication Data

Gottfried, Ted.
    Marijuana / by Ted Gottfried with Lisa Harkrader.
        p. cm. — (Benchmark rockets : drug facts)
    Includes index.
    Summary: "Discusses the history, effects, and dangers of Marijuana as well
as addiction treatment options"—Provided by publisher.
    ISBN 978-0-7614-4351-3
1. Marijuana—History—Juvenile literature. 2. Cannabis—History—Juvenile
literature. I. Harkrader, Lisa. II. Title.

HV5822.M3G685 2010
613.8'35—dc22
2008052761

Publisher: Michelle Bisson
Editorial Development and Book Design: Trillium Publishing, Inc.

Photo research by Trillium Publishing, Inc.

Cover photo: Shutterstock.com/itay uri

The photographs and illustrations in this book are used by permission and
through the courtesy of: Shutterstock.com: Jan van der Hoeven, 1; John Lumb,
10; Diego Cervo, 14; Gelpi, 18. iStockphoto.com: Karin Lau, 5; Craig Cozart, 15;
lillisphotography, 27. AP Photo: Robert W. Klein, 7. Getty Images: Lawrence Lucier,
9. Ronald Reagan Library: 17. Orange County NORML: 23. Muskogee Phoenix: 25.

Printed in Malaysia
1 3 5 6 4 2

CONTENTS

1 A Look at Marijuana

MARIJUANA IS THE MOST COMMONLY USED ILLEGAL drug in the United States. People have different opinions about marijuana. Some argue that the drug should be legal for medical uses. Some argue that it should be legal for even broader use. Others say marijuana is too dangerous to be legal for any reason.

But one thing everyone can agree on is that right now, in the United States, marijuana is illegal according to federal law. You can go to jail for using it. You can go to jail for having it in your possession. You can go to jail for selling it.

The Indian Hemp Plant

Marijuana comes from a plant called Indian hemp. Varieties of hemp grow in temperate climates all over the world. A **resin** in the hemp plant contains **THC** (tetrahydrocannabinol). THC is a chemical in hemp that is responsible for the effects marijuana has on **users**. It changes the way the brain works. All of the parts of the plant—including the leaves, seeds, stems, bark, and flowering tops—contain THC.

Hashish is the strongest form of marijuana. Often called "hash," it is eight times stronger than the average marijuana used in the United States. Hashish is **distilled** from the resin of the Indian hemp plant and looks like a brown lump of powder.

Marijuana Facts

Marijuana has more than two hundred slang names, including:

- Pot
- Herb
- Weed
- Boom
- Gangster
- Mary Jane

A marijuana cigarette is sometimes called a:

- Joint
- Reefer
- Doobie
- Roach

The marijuana plant is also called the Indian hemp plant. It grows wild in dry areas with mild climates.

Marijuana can have many effects on a user, including:

- Feeling relaxed or high
- Having a strong thirst or hunger
- Feeling anxious or paranoid

The effects of marijuana depend on many factors, including:

- The user's mood, age, health, and previous experience with the drug
- How much THC the marijuana contains
- The location where the drug is used
- How the drug is taken
- Whether the user is also drinking alcohol or using other drugs

A Major Crop

The hemp plant has not always been illegal. In fact, it hasn't always been used as a drug. Hemp was a major crop for American colonists. They used it to make paper, clothing, and rope. Many of our nation's founders, including George Washington, grew hemp. It was so important to the economy that the colony of Virginia passed a law imposing penalties on farms that did not grow hemp.

The invention of the cotton gin in 1793 meant the end of hemp as an American crop. With the cotton gin, farmers could more easily separate cotton fiber from the cotton plant. Cotton became cheaper to produce than hemp. Many hemp plantations switched to growing cotton. After the Civil War, other hemp plantations began to grow tobacco instead.

A Move to Medicine

Although people no longer used hemp for paper or clothing, its use as a medicine increased. People swallowed it as a syrup. THC in syrup form is stronger than in the dried form that people smoke. People used the syrup to treat many health problems, including gout, migraines, depression, loss of appetite, and childbirth pains.

One problem with using marijuana as a medicine was that the amount of THC in the syrup was hard to control. Different varieties of hemp contain different levels of THC, so different syrups had different strengths. The syrup also affected different people in different ways. By the early 1900s, marijuana's use as a medicine began to decline.

Marijuana as a Recreational Drug

Although marijuana's use as a medicine was declining, people continued to use it as a **recreational drug**. During the 1920s, special places called tea pads were set up where people could smoke marijuana and relax. By 1930, there were five hundred of these places in New York City alone. Marijuana became illegal in most states by the end of the 1930s, but its use has continued to grow.

Young people who smoked marijuana in the 1960s were called "flower children." They were against the war in Vietnam, and their slogan was "Make love, not war."

7

2 Highs and Lows

THERE SEEMS TO BE NO ONE ANSWER AS TO WHAT THE effects of smoking marijuana are. However, people have reached conclusions that need to be considered in order to understand how marijuana does or does not affect people.

Not a Pretty Picture

The National Institute on Drug Abuse (NIDA) of the U.S. Department of Health and Human Services says that THC quickly passes from the lungs into the bloodstream when someone smokes marijuana. Blood carries THC to organs throughout the body, including the brain. THC acts on certain nerve cells in the brain, which affects the user's concentration, thoughts, coordination, and sense of time and pleasure.

NIDA says that short-term effects may include memory blocks, learning problems, distorted perception, unstable blood pressure, and increased heart rate. According to NIDA, long-term smoking of marijuana can also damage the lungs. A 1993 study found that frequent marijuana smokers had more health problems and missed more days of work than those who did not smoke the drug. NIDA also claims that continual smoking of marijuana increases a user's risk of lung infection and blocked airways.

NIDA believes a more serious problem is the risk of lung cancer. Marijuana smoke contains 50 to 70 percent more cancer-causing chemicals than tobacco smoke. Marijuana smokers also tend to inhale more deeply and wait longer to exhale. NIDA says that this increases their exposure to cancer-causing smoke.

On the Other Hand . . .

Critics point out that NIDA's focus is the abuse of drugs. They say the studies ignore people who control their marijuana use and suffer few ill effects. They note that although marijuana can increase heart rate, little evidence links it to heart attacks.

Critics remind us that many other widely used substances can cause health problems. Salt can raise blood pressure. Coffee, tea, and sodas that contain caffeine can cause nervousness and interrupt sleep. Caffeine can also cause breathing problems and bone loss. Sugar contributes to obesity, diabetes, and dental cavities. Nutmeg and some other spices can affect the nervous system.

Dr. Andrew Weil disagrees with NIDA's conclusions on marijuana.

Dr. Andrew Weil has studied drugs for over 40 years. He points out that marijuana is not like other drugs. It's neither a **hallucinogen** nor a **stimulant**. Weil agrees that smoking marijuana causes a mild increase in heart rate, redness of the eyes, and dryness in the throat and mouth. Weil also says that other so-called effects of smoking marijuana have not been proven.

The Canadian Medical Association and a British scientific panel agree that marijuana use is not associated with major health problems. *The Lancet*, a leading medical journal, says "the smoking of **cannabis**, even long-term, is not harmful to health."

A Mood-Altering Drug

Whether marijuana is harmful remains an open question. However, there is no doubt that marijuana affects the brain and changes the user's behavior. Short-term effects of the drug may include:

Smoking marijuana can cause dreaminess.

- A sense of well-being
- Talkativeness and giggles
- Dizziness
- Dreaminess
- Difficulty walking
- Memory problems
- Sluggishness

Frequent use can also have long-term effects. NIDA reports that workers who are regular marijuana users were more likely to goof off and leave work without permission. According to the Mayo Health Clinic, users may have trouble paying attention even 24 hours after using the drug.

Young marijuana smokers may have trouble focusing in class. They may withdraw from family and friends.

Opinions on Marijuana Use

Harmful

[It has a] lasting effect. Even after a day of not using marijuana, adverse cognitive effects—such as problems paying attention—can still be detected in heavy users of marijuana.

—*Mayo Health Clinic*

Long-term marijuana use can lead to addiction for some people; that is, they use the drug compulsively even though it often interferes with family, school, work, and recreational activities; craving and withdrawal symptoms can make it hard for long-term marijuana smokers to stop using the drug.

—*National Institute on Drug Abuse*

Not Harmful

In strict medical terms marijuana is far safer than many foods we commonly consume. It is physically impossible to eat enough marijuana to induce death. Marijuana, in its natural form, is one of the safest therapeutically active substances known to man.

—*Francis L. Young, administrative law judge of the U.S. Drug Enforcement Administration*

By any of the major criteria of harm—mortality, morbidity, toxicity, addictiveness and relationship with crime—[cannabis] is less harmful than any of the major illicit drugs, or than alcohol or tobacco.

—*March 2000 Report of the British Police Foundation*

Dangerous Combination

A group called the Drug Abuse Warning Network (DAWN) tracks drug-related deaths and injuries. In 2001, DAWN found that marijuana was a factor in more than 110,000 emergency visits to hospitals in the United States. Another center for health research found that daily marijuana users had a 30 percent higher risk of injuries from accidents than nonusers.

Even Dr. Dale Gieringer of the National Organization for the Reform of Marijuana Laws (NORML) warns that "accidents are probably the number one hazard of marijuana" and that marijuana affects "judgment and coordination at complex tasks including driving."

Dr. Gieringer points out that at least half of the drivers involved in fatal auto accidents had been drinking, while between 7 and 20 percent had been using marijuana. Of those, 70 to 90 percent also had alcohol in their blood. The National Highway Traffic Safety Administration (NHTSA) studied accidents that involved both alcohol and marijuana. They reported that alcohol was by far the major cause of those accidents. NHTSA found that the effects of marijuana on driving seem to be less than those of alcohol. Unlike alcohol, marijuana seems to make drivers more cautious. This may be because marijuana smokers are more aware of their condition and try to make up for it.

Still, the effects of marijuana are different from person to person. The younger and less experienced the driver is, the more likely marijuana will affect his or her judgment behind the wheel.

Is Marijuana Addictive?

Not only are there questions about whether marijuana is harmful, there are also questions about whether it is **addictive**. Are frequent marijuana users able to control their use of the drug? Are they unable to stop using it?

The World Health Organization describes the differences between drugs that are addictive and drugs that are habit forming.

Addictive Drugs	Habit-Forming Drugs
• Cause an irresistible need for the drug • Cause users to become more and more tolerant of the drug's effects • Cannot be withdrawn without causing severe and painful physical symptoms	• Create an emotional or psychological need for the drug • Can be withdrawn without causing physical harm or pain

Most experts agree that marijuana is not physically addictive, but it can cause psychological dependency in some cases. NIDA points out that long-term users continue to smoke marijuana even though they know it interferes with family, school, work, and activities.

Experts also agree that it is not easy to stop smoking marijuana. When users give up marijuana, they can suffer from:

- Cravings for the drug
- Sleeplessness
- Anxiety
- Aggression
- Depression
- Loss of appetite

When some users stop smoking marijuana, they suffer from depression.

Is Marijuana a Gateway Drug?

Many people believe that marijuana is a **gateway drug**—that it leads users to take harder, more dangerous drugs, such as cocaine, Ecstasy, and heroin.

A 2003 study found that teens who began using marijuana by age 17 were more likely to use other drugs. This study suggests that heavy marijuana use may cause the brain to release a certain chemical. This chemical could affect the brain in a way that makes the brain more easily affected by other drugs. NIDA warns that "the risk of using cocaine is much greater for those who have tried marijuana." Some users themselves report that smoking marijuana led them to experiment with other drugs.

The World Health Organization (WHO) reports that their studies showed no evidence that marijuana leads to heroin use. The Institute of Medicine in Washington, D.C., found no clear evidence that marijuana caused later abuse of other drugs. In 2002, a report by the British government concluded that the incidence of marijuana leading to harder drugs "is found to be very small."

What does this conflicting research tell us? Is marijuana a gateway drug? A study in the *Journal of the American Medical Association* suggests three possible explanations:

- People who find marijuana pleasurable may experiment with other drugs that promise greater pleasure.

- Even though marijuana is illegal, most marijuana smokers have not suffered legal consequences. They may believe that using other drugs will not lead to punishment either.

- The most common experience is that because marijuana is illegal, users must buy marijuana from drug dealers. These dealers also sell hard drugs and promise users even bigger highs than marijuana can give.

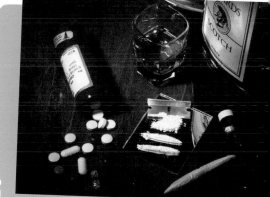

Besides marijuana, drug dealers sell hard drugs, such as Ecstasy or heroin.

The bottom line seems to be that marijuana *can* be a gateway drug, but it doesn't *have* to be.

3 Go Directly to Jail

The Army's Campaign

In the 1960s, American troops came into contact with marijuana while fighting in Vietnam. In Vietnam, marijuana was cheap and easy to get. Smoking marijuana became so common among American troops that the army began an all-out campaign to stop its use. They made mass arrests of soldiers found with marijuana.

Two years later, the U.S. Department of Defense found that the crackdown had been very effective. Marijuana use among the troops had greatly decreased. They also found an unexpected result. Soldiers who stopped using marijuana had started using heroin. Heroin was also cheap and easy to get. It was odorless and less bulky than marijuana, making it harder to detect. Heroin was also extremely addictive and far more dangerous than marijuana.

The Crackdown

Marijuana use increased during the 1960s. Young people used marijuana more openly, smoking it at concerts and war protests. Many people were outraged. They blamed marijuana for firing up rebels on college campuses and causing race riots in inner cities. Although using, possessing, and selling marijuana had been a crime in the United States for decades, now the government began cracking down on marijuana violations as it never had before.

By 1968, the widespread use of marijuana had become a political issue. Two months before he was elected president, Richard Nixon gave a speech launching the War on Drugs.

At first, marijuana users did not take the War on Drugs seriously. They still got together in parks and on college campuses to smoke marijuana. In 1969, about 400,000 people gathered on a dairy farm in Bethel, New York, for a three-day music festival called Woodstock. Through clouds of marijuana smoke, cameras caught people streaking, making out, and using drugs. The public was appalled. The government passed even harsher drug laws.

In the early 1980s, President Ronald Reagan decided that marijuana should be the main target of the War on Drugs. In 1984, the president's wife, Nancy Reagan, spoke to an elementary school in California. She told the students to "Just say no" to smoking marijuana. This became the slogan of the War on Drugs for the next 20 years.

Former first lady Nancy Reagan spoke at a "Just Say No!" rally on May 22, 1986 at the White House.

Mandatory Sentencing

In 1986, Congress passed a law creating **mandatory** sentences in drug cases. Anyone arrested with 100 kilograms of marijuana faced five years in jail without parole. For 1,000 kilograms or more, a person faced ten years. The jail time increased for second offenses. For third offenses, the sentence was life in prison.

In 1988, a second law made everyone involved in selling drugs responsible for the crime. A dealer's lookout could receive the same punishment as the drug **cartel**'s leader.

The prison population swelled. From 1986 to 1998, the number of drug offenders in federal prisons rose 450 percent. Inga Parsons of the New York University School of Law says: "It's the person caught holding the bag, who usually is the poorest . . . They are the ones most likely to be convicted."

Jerry G.

One person caught up in the War on Drugs was Jerry G., a 19-year-old college student. To pledge a school fraternity, Jerry was told to buy a kilo of marijuana. The dealer turned out to be an undercover officer. Jerry was arrested and sentenced to prison. "Because I had a whole kilo, they said I must be a pusher," says Jerry. "But . . . I wasn't selling the stuff." He served several years in prison. Now, he can't afford to go back to college and is having trouble finding a job.

The Issue of Legalizing Marijuana

In a 2001 survey, more than 83 million Americans said they had tried marijuana. Many people believe the War on Drugs has contributed to the increase in marijuana use. They think a better approach is to **legalize** marijuana.

In 1970, Keith Stroup founded the National Organization for the Reform of Marijuana Laws (NORML). NORML's goal is to make responsible use of cannabis by adults no longer a crime. NORML claims marijuana is far less harmful than alcohol and tobacco. It says legalizing marijuana would:

- Reduce costs to law enforcement agencies
- Reduce contact between marijuana smokers and hard drug dealers
- Reduce violence among street gangs that fight turf wars over where they can sell marijuana
- Allow marijuana sales to be licensed and regulated, as tobacco and alcohol are
- Keep marijuana out of the hands of minors

Some people feel we should legalize all drugs. In 1993, U.S. Surgeon General Jocelyn Elders was fired for saying that we should do studies on drug legalization. In 1998, a two-page letter in the *New York Times* argued for drug legalization. More than 150 important Americans signed the letter.

Marijuana Timeline

3000 BC   The earliest known use of marijuana takes place in China and Central Asia.

1762   Virginia colony passes a law imposing penalties on farms that do not grow hemp.

1854   *United States Pharmacopeia* includes marijuana in its list of medicines.

1920–   Prohibition in the U.S. banned alcohol. Marijuana was legal,
1933   and its use grew.

1937   The U.S. passes the federal Marihuana Tax Act, making marijuana illegal.

1968   Congress creates the Law Enforcement Assistance Administration to fight crime and street violence. Drugs—especially marijuana—become its main target.

Presidential candidate Richard Nixon proclaims a War on Drugs.

1969   Woodstock music festival fuels more public outrage against marijuana.

1970   NORML (National Organization for the Reform of Marijuana Laws) is founded.

1973   New York legislature passes laws imposing harsh penalties for drug trafficking.

1980s   The Reagan administration focuses the War on Drugs on marijuana.

The book *Toughlove* urges parents to treat pot-smoking children as criminals.

1984   Nancy Reagan introduces "Just Say No!" as the slogan of the War on Drugs.

1988   Congress passes the Anti-Drug Abuse Act, creating mandatory sentences in drug cases.

Congress passes a second Anti-Drug Abuse Act, requiring employers doing business with the federal government to maintain a drug-free workplace.

1993   Surgeon General Jocelyn Elders is fired for making remarks that supported the study of the legalization of drugs.

1995   U.S. Supreme Court upholds a school's right to test student athletes for drugs.

1996   California and Arizona become the first states to legalize medical marijuana.

Arizona initiative overturned by the state legislature.

1998   A letter in the *New York Times*, signed by 150 prominent Americans, proclaims that the War on Drugs causes more harm than drug abuse itself.

2000   The National Association of Criminal Defense Lawyers calls for the **decriminalization** of all drugs.

2008   Michigan joins the states of Alaska, California, Hawaii, Maine, Montana, Nevada, New Mexico, Oregon, Rhode Island, Vermont, and Washington in passing laws that make medical marijuana legal.

Massachusetts joins the states of Alaska, California, Colorado, Maine, Minnesota, Mississippi, Nebraska, Nevada, New York, North Carolina, Ohio, and Oregon to decriminalize the personal possession of small amounts of marijuana.

The Establishment Position

The Drug Enforcement Administration (DEA) argues that the War on Drugs has been a success. It says drug use in the U.S. has gone down by one-third in the last 20 years. It says that marijuana is harmful and that society would be at risk if it were easily available. The DEA points out that the level of THC in marijuana is higher today than it was in the 1970s. It stresses the link between drugs, crime, and violence.

Medical Marijuana

Many people want to legalize marijuana for medical use. Cancer patients often experience dizziness and nausea during treatment. AIDS drugs cause nausea, stomach cramps, and joint pain. Many people say smoking marijuana can help ease these symptoms. Marijuana may also be useful in treating other diseases such as glaucoma, multiple sclerosis, epilepsy, and chronic pain.

In 1997, the National Academy of Sciences agreed that marijuana may help people with cancer and AIDS. It also warned that smoking marijuana might cause lung cancer and other health problems. Polls show that 80 percent of Americans believe medical marijuana should be legal. In 1996, voters in California and Arizona voted to permit marijuana for medical use. While the state legislature of Arizona overturned this initiative, other states have followed California's lead to legalize marijuana for medical use.

A group campaigns for the legalization of marijuana.

The federal government under President George W. Bush insisted that federal law overrules state laws. Federal law does not permit marijuana use for medical reasons. AIDS and cancer patients can find themselves trapped between state and federal law. Even if their state allows medical marijuana use, they can still be arrested under federal law.

The DEA does agree that smoking marijuana may relieve symptoms for some cancer and AIDS cases. They say, however, that patients can get the same results from a **synthetic** form of THC which doctors can prescribe. Since it is not smoked, it does not cause lung damage. However, these pills can be expensive, hard to get, and slow-acting. In contrast, marijuana is much cheaper and provides quick relief.

4 Taking the Test

PARENTS HAVE THE RIGHT TO LOOK OUT FOR THEIR children's welfare. The law says that school authorities also have the right to act in place of a parent at school.

In 1995, the U.S. Supreme Court upheld a school's right to test student athletes for drugs. The Court said that students who chose to participate in school athletics should expect intrusions on their rights and their privacy. A 2002 Supreme Court decision gave schools the right to test students taking part in any **extracurricular** activities.

Reasons for Testing

Many people favor drug testing because they are concerned about the effects on students who smoke marijuana. A NIDA survey shows that students who smoke marijuana:

- Get lower grades
- Are less likely to graduate
- Score lower on tests
- Have problems with attention, memory, and learning

Another reason for concern is that smoking marijuana affects a person's driving ability. The effects vary from driver to driver, but they are greatest for inexperienced teen drivers. Supporters of drug tests say that if testing keeps students affected by marijuana from driving, it can save lives.

Supporters of drug testing often link marijuana use with violence. The smoking of marijuana is usually not linked to violence, but students who buy marijuana on the street do come into contact with drug dealers. These dealers often urge marijuana smokers to try other drugs. Then students can be drawn into a world of crime and violence.

School authorities have the right to search for drugs in students' lockers.

The Testing Process

Schools use different methods to detect drugs. Some test students' urine, blood, hair, and/or saliva. Some also bring in drug-sniffing dogs.

NIDA approves urine testing to determine if a student has used marijuana. Tests can detect THC in the urine for two to three days after the person has inhaled or swallowed marijuana. For regular users, tests can detect THC for up to 12 weeks. If a test shows evidence of marijuana, a second test is done to confirm the results.

Does Punishment Work?

What happens to students who fail drug tests? Although many believe they should go into treatment programs, there aren't enough programs to fill the need. Instead, most offending students face punishment. Punishment usually means the student gets expelled from school.

A group called Teachers Against Prohibition points out that involvement in extracurricular school activities discourages drug use. They say that expelling marijuana users will create "drug-using dropouts." They believe testing may force marijuana smokers to switch to harder drugs that are more difficult to detect.

Does Testing Work?

The purpose of testing is to keep students from using drugs. Superintendent Lisa Brady of Hunterdon Central Regional High School in New Jersey believes it works. In 1997, Hunterdon began testing student athletes. By 1999, the number of tenth graders using drugs or alcohol dropped from 47.3 to 41.8 percent. Brady believes testing caused the reduced drug use.

Others disagree that testing works. The American Civil Liberties Union (ACLU) believes that drug testing is often inaccurate. The group believes there is no proof that drug testing has discouraged drug use. Several studies support this view. These studies find that drug testing in schools does not discourage marijuana use any more than no testing at all.

Why Smoke At All?

Peer pressure is the main reason young people use marijuana. Most kids have heard the sneers and coaxing: *Don't be a chicken! You're such a baby! It'll make you feel great! Everybody's doing it!* Peer pressure works because most teens want to be accepted by a group, even when the group is going down the wrong path.

Some young people smoke marijuana because their older brothers and sisters do. Some see people smoking on TV and in movies and hear songs about it. They decide that smoking marijuana must be cool. Some teens use marijuana to escape their problems. Marijuana doesn't cause suicide, but teens with emotional problems are more likely to use marijuana and consider suicide.

In the End

How America deals with marijuana is changing. More states are permitting the use of medical marijuana. Overcrowded prisons are pushing states to rethink harsh sentences for marijuana offenses. Public opinion is shifting toward easing restrictions on marijuana use.

In many neighborhoods, signs like this one warn drug dealers to keep away.

Whatever reforms we make, nearly everyone agrees marijuana should be kept out of the hands of minors. Minors lack the maturity to use drugs, such as marijuana, that affect the brain. There are age limits for drinking, smoking cigarettes, and driving. Many think we also need an age limit if marijuana becomes legal.

One joint won't kill a user, but one joint too many may. When teens begin considering what they may gain by smoking marijuana, they should also consider how much they could lose.

27

GLOSSARY

addictive: Something that causes a person to become dependent on it physically and/or mentally.

cannabis: The hemp plant that produces marijuana and hashish, scientific name *cannabis sativa*. Also the name used for the syrup form of marijuana used as a medicine.

cartel: An international group formed to control prices and the selling of a product such as drugs.

decriminalization: The removal of penalties for producing or selling a drug.

distilled: The process of heating a liquid or solid until it sends off a gas; then cooling the gas until it becomes liquid.

extracurricular: School activities such as sports or drama which are outside the regular school program.

gateway drug: A "soft" drug, such as marijuana, that can lead to the use of more dangerous drugs, like heroin.

hallucinogen: A drug that causes users to see objects or experience feelings that are not real.

hashish: The most potent form of marijuana.

legalize: To make legal; to repeal laws banning the sale and possession of all drugs or some specific drugs, such as marijuana or medical marijuana.

mandatory: Required by authorities.

peer pressure: Pressure by fellow minors to join in unwise activities such as smoking marijuana.

recreational drug: A substance that's used for pleasure rather than out of medical need; also a term for the occasional use of an illegal drug, such as on weekends only.

resin: A yellowish or brownish substance that comes from the sap of some plants.

stimulant: A drug that makes the body or one of its parts more active.

synthetic: Produced in a lab by people.

THC (tetrahydrocannabinol): The active chemical in marijuana that is responsible for the intoxicating effect on the user.

users: People who regularly smoke marijuana or use other drugs.

FIND OUT MORE

Books

Axelrod-Contrada, Joan. *The Facts about Drugs and Society*. New York: Marshall Cavendish, 2008.

Gottfried, Ted. *The Facts about Marijuana*. New York: Marshall Cavendish, 2005.

Websites

Drug Enforcement Administration (DEA)
http://www.usdoj.gov/dea

Marijuana Policy Project (MPP)
http://www.mpp.org

National Council on Alcoholism and Drug Dependence (NCADD)
http://www.ncadd.org

National Institute on Drug Abuse (NIDA)
http://www.nida.nih.gov

National Organization for the Reform of Marijuana Laws (NORML)
http://www.norml.org

Office of National Drug Control Policy (ONDCP)
http://www.whitehousedrugpolicy.gov

Partnership for a Drug-Free America
http://www.drugfreeamerica.org

SAMHSA's National Clearinghouse for Alcohol and Drug Information (NCADI)
http://www.samhsa.gov/centers/csap/csap.html

INDEX

Page numbers for photographs and illustrations are in **boldface**.

mandatory sentencing, 18,
21
Marihuana Tax Act, 20
Mayo Clinic, 10
medical use, 4, 6, 21, 22, 23,
27

National Association of
Criminal Defense Lawyers,
21
National Institute on Drug
Abuse (NIDA), 8, 9, 10, 11,
13, 14, 24, 25
National Highway Traffic
Safety Administration
(NHTSA), 12
National Organization for
the Reform of Marijuana
Laws (NORML), 12, 19, 20
New York Times, 19, 21
Nixon, President Richard,
17, 20

peer pressure, 26
prison population, 18
Prohibition, 20, 26
punishment, 25

Reagan, Nancy, 17, **17**, 20
Reagan, President Ronald,
17, 20
recreational drug, 7

slang terms for marijuana, 5
stimulant, 9
Stroup, Keith, 19
Teachers Against Prohibition,
26
THC (tetrahydrocannabinol),
4, 5, 6, 8, 22, 23, 25

U.S. Supreme Court, 21, 24
urine testing, 25

Vietnam, 7, 16

War on Drugs, 17, 19, 20, 21,
22
Washington, George, 6
Weil, Dr. Andrew, 9, **9**
Woodstock, 17, 20
World Health Organization
(WHO), 13, 14